MLB's Greatest Teams

CHICAGO CUBS

Big Buddy Books
An Imprint of Abdo Publishing
abdopublishing.com

Katie Lajiness

abdopublishing.com

Published by Abdo Publishing, a division of ABDO, PO Box 398166, Minneapolis, Minnesota 55439.
Copyright © 2019 by Abdo Consulting Group, Inc. International copyrights reserved in all countries. No part
of this book may be reproduced in any form without written permission from the publisher. Big Buddy Books™
is a trademark and logo of Abdo Publishing.

Printed in the United States of America, North Mankato, Minnesota.
052018
092018

THIS BOOK CONTAINS
RECYCLED MATERIALS

Cover Photo: Jamie Squire/Getty Images.
Interior Photos: 33ft/Depositphotos (p. 7); AP Images (p. 22); AT History/Alamy Stock Photo (p. 19); Brian
    Kersey/Getty Images (p. 5); David Banks/Getty Images (p. 28); Everett Collection Historical/Alamy Stock
    Photo (p. 11); Jamie Squire/Getty Images (pp. 24, 25, 29); Jim Palmer/AP Images (p. 15); John Cordes/AP
    Images (p. 23); John Swart/AP Images (p. 17); Jonathan Daniel/Getty Images (pp. 9, 27); Otto Greule Jr/
    Getty Images (p. 23); Paul Fearn/Alamy Stock Photo (p. 13); Robert H. Houston/AP Images (p. 22); Scott
    Cunningham/Getty Images (p. 21).

Coordinating Series Editor: Tamara L. Britton
Graphic Design: Jenny Christensen

Library of Congress Control Number: 2017962670

Publisher's Cataloging-in-Publication Data

Names: Lajiness, Katie, author.
Title: Chicago Cubs / by Katie Lajiness.
Description: Minneapolis, Minnesota : Abdo Publishing, 2019. | Series: MLB's greatest
    teams | Includes online resources and index.
Identifiers: ISBN 9781532115158 (lib.bdg.) | ISBN 9781532155871 (ebook)
Subjects: LCSH: Major League Baseball (Organization)--Juvenile literature. | Baseball
    teams--United States--History--Juvenile literature. | Chicago Cubs (Baseball team)--
    Juvenile literature. | Sports teams--Juvenile literature.
Classification: DDC 796.35764--dc23

Contents

Major League Baseball 4

A Winning Team. 6

Wrigley Field 8

Then and Now. 10

Highlights 14

Famous Managers 18

Star Players 22

Final Call 26

Through the Years. 28

Glossary 30

Online Resources 31

Index 32

Major League Baseball

League Pla

There are two
leagues in MLB. They
the American League (AL)
National League (NL). Eac
has 15 teams and is sp
three divisions. The
are east, central,
and west.

The Chicago Cubs is one of 30 Major League Baseball (MLB) teams. The team plays in the National League Central **Division**.
Throughout the season, all MLB teams play 162 games. The season begins in April and can continue until November.

The Cubs mascot is named Clark because Wrigley Field is on Clark Street.

A Winning Team

The Cubs team is from Chicago, Illinois. The team's colors are red, white, and blue.

The team has had good seasons and bad. But time and again, the Cubs players have proven themselves. Let's see what makes the Cubs one of MLB's greatest teams!

Fast Facts

HOME FIELD: Wrigley Field

TEAM COLORS: Red, white, and blue

TEAM SONG: "Go, Cubs, Go" by Steve Goodman

PENNANTS: 17

WORLD SERIES TITLES: 1907, 1908, 2016

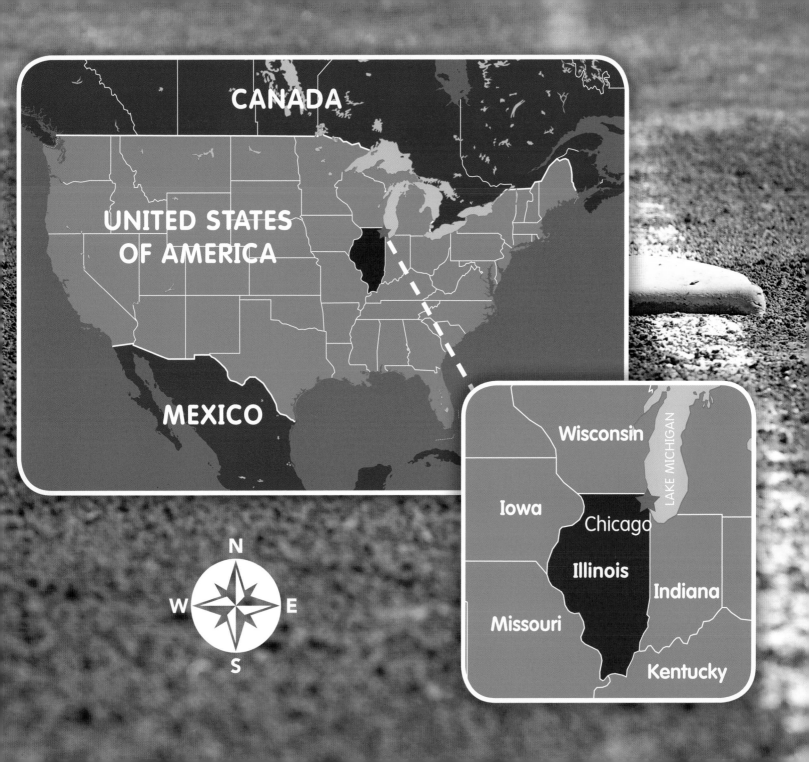

Wrigley Field

From 1876 to 1915, the Cubs played in five different parks. The team moved to its final home in 1916. The ballpark was called Weeghman Park. The name changed to Cubs Park in 1920.

Finally in 1926, the name became Wrigley Field. Today, it is the second-oldest baseball stadium that is still in use.

The Cubs play against four other teams in the Central Division. They are the Cincinnati Reds, the Milwaukee Brewers, the St. Louis Cardinals, and the Pittsburgh Pirates.

Then and Now

Starting out, the team went by the name Chicago White Stockings. William Hulbert became owner of the team after the **Great Fire of 1871**.

Hulbert and other team owners started a new baseball league in 1876. It was called the National League and it still exists today. Hulbert was president of the league until he died in 1882.

COPYRIGHTED 1895 BY
K FOX POLICE GAZETTE, NEW Y

VOL. LXVI– Nº 926
SUPPLEMENT TO THE
POLICE GAZETTE
JUNE 1ST 1895.
RICHARD K. FOX. PROPR.

OUR BASEBALL HEROES.

CAPTAINS OF THE TWELVE CLUBS IN THE NATIONAL LEAGUE.

The NL began in 1876 and the AL began in 1901. The two leagues played together in the first World Series in 1903.

Later, a writer from the *Chicago Daily News* said the team had many young players. He called the players "cubs" in a news article. The name stuck. It became the team's official name in 1907.

Over the years, the team used a few different names. Members have played as the White Stockings, the Colts, and the Orphans.

Highlights

The Cubs' best season was in 1906. That year, the team won 116 games. The team won its first two World Series in 1907 and 1908.

Later, the Cubs won three NL **pennants** during the 1910s and 1920s. Then from 1929 to 1938, the Cubs led the NL with four pennants.

For many years, the Cubs players continued to play their best. The team was first in the NL Eastern **Division** for most of the 1969 season.

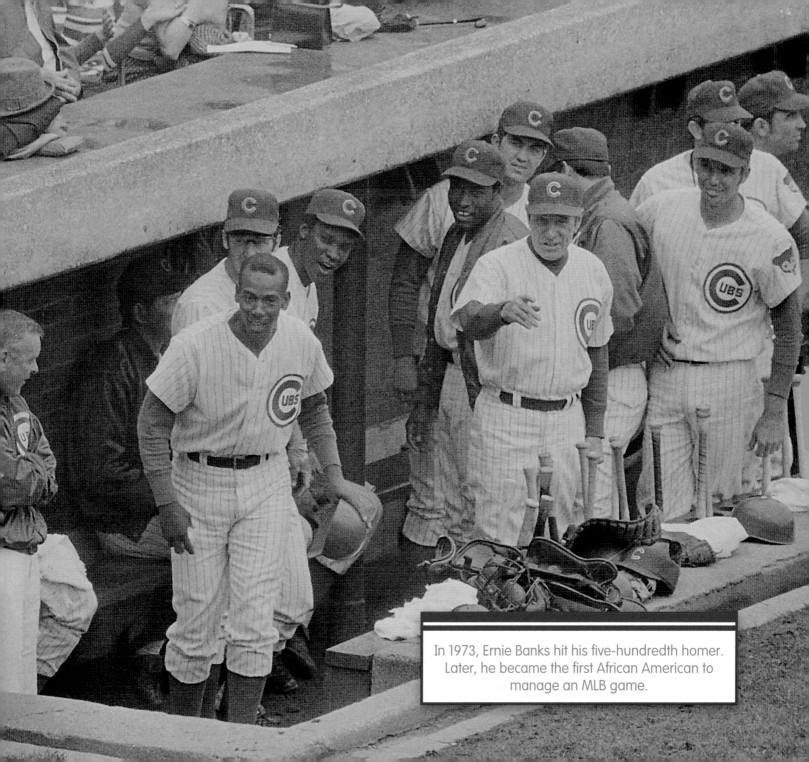

In 1973, Ernie Banks hit his five-hundredth homer. Later, he became the first African American to manage an MLB game.

In 2007 and 2008, the Cubs won two NL Central **Division** titles. It was only the second team in MLB history to record 10,000 wins.

Finally in 2016, the Cubs won the World Series after more than 100 years! In total, the team has won 17 NL **pennants** and three World Series titles.

From 1982 to 1997, sports announcer
Harry Caray led the fans in singing
"Take Me Out to the Ballgame."

Famous Managers

Frank Chance was a successful baseball player and manager. From 1906 to 1910, Chance led the Cubs to four **pennant** wins. The team won the World Series in 1907 and again in 1908.

Chance was one of the greatest managers in team history. The team earned 768 wins during his eight years as Cubs manager.

Chance led his team to 100 wins in four-out-of-seven full seasons. Under his command, the Cubs never finished lower than third place in the NL.

In 2014, Joe Maddon became the fifty-fourth manager in Cubs history. The following year, he earned the title of NL Manager of the Year.

In 2016, Maddon led the team to its first World Series win in 108 years. His management style helped the team win 200 games in back-to-back seasons.

Before the Cubs, Maddon managed the Tampa Bay Rays and the Anaheim Angels.

Star Players

Ernie Banks FIRST BASEMAN, #14

1953 – 1971

In 1953, Ernie Banks joined the team as the Cubs' first African-American player. A natural **athlete**, Banks won a **Most Valuable Player (MVP)** Award in 1958 and 1959. And he won the **Gold Glove Award** in 1960. Banks was **inducted** into the National Baseball Hall of Fame in 1977.

Ron Santo THIRD BASEMAN, #10

During Ron Santo's 14 seasons with the Cubs, he won five Gold Glove Awards. Throughout his **career**, he played in nine All-Star Games. And he won the Lou Gehrig Memorial Award. In 2003, the Cubs **retired** the number 10 jersey in Santo's honor. He was inducted into the National Baseball Hall of Fame in 2012.

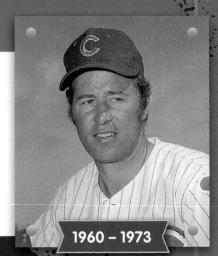

1960 – 1973

Ryne Sandberg SECOND BASEMAN, #23

In 1984, Ryne Sandberg led the league with 114 runs and 19 **triples**. He won an NL **MVP** Award and he was part of ten-straight All-Star Games. When he **retired** in 1997, Sandberg had hit more home runs than any second baseman in history. He was **inducted** into the National Baseball Hall of Fame in 2005.

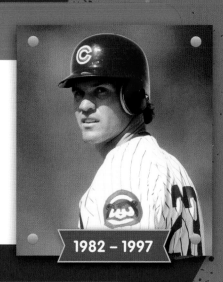

1982 – 1997

Sammy Sosa RIGHT FIELDER, #21

In the famous 1998 home run chase, Sammy Sosa knocked 66 homers out of the park. As a result, he won *Sports Illustrated* Sportsperson of the Year alongside Mark McGwire. That year, he also won the NL MVP Award.

1992 – 2004

23

Anthony Rizzo FIRST BASEMAN, #44

2012 –

Anthony Rizzo overcame an illness called cancer to play in MLB. He became the first Cubs player to earn three game-winning **runs batted in (RBIs)** in his first five games. As of 2017, Rizzo has twice been named the NL's Player of the Week. And he has been part of three All-Star Games.

Jake Arrieta PITCHER, #49

In July 2015, Jake Arrieta pitched a complete game win over the Chicago White Sox. This was the third complete game of his MLB **career**. That year, Arrieta won the NL Cy Young Award. And in 2016, he won the **Silver Slugger Award** for pitchers.

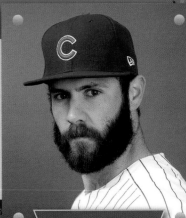

2013 –

Kris Bryant THIRD BASEMAN, #17

Kris Bryant has been winning awards since he was in college. In 2013, he won Baseball America's College Player of the Year Award. One year later, he won the Minor League Player of the Year Award. And in 2015, he won Baseball America's **Rookie** of the Year Award. Finally, he earned the NL **MVP** Award in 2016.

2013 –

Javier Baez SECOND BASEMAN, #9

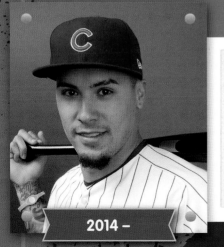

2014 –

After a few years in the minor leagues, Javier Baez began playing with the Cubs. In 2016, he was named MVP of the NL **Championship** Series. And, he helped the Cubs win the 2016 World Series. Baez played in the 2017 World Baseball Classic for Puerto Rico, his home country.

25

Final Call

The Chicago Cubs have a long, rich history. The team has played in 11 World Series and won three.

Even during losing seasons, true fans have stuck by the team's players. Many believe the Cubs will remain one of the greatest teams in MLB.

All-Stars

The best players from both leagues come together each year for the All-Star Game. This game does not count toward the regular season records. It is simply to celebrate the best players in MLB.

The Cubs played the Cleveland Indians in the 2016 World Series. In Game Seven, Chicago won 8–7.

Through the Years

1916

The Cubs moved from Chicago's West Side to the North Side Park. It would later be called Wrigley Field.

1929

The Cubs lost 3–1 to Philadelphia in the World Series at Wrigley Field.

1937

Outfield walls were covered in ivy to make the stadium look like a park. The ivy has been part of the ballpark ever since.

1945

The Cubs took the NL **pennant** with 98 wins.

1948

The first Cubs game was **broadcast** on television.

1988

The Cubs played the first night game at Wrigley Field.

1999

Sammy Sosa became the first player in MLB to hit 60 home runs in back-to-back seasons.

2003

The Cubs were close to the World Series for the first time since 1945. They lost the NL **Championship** Series to the Florida Marlins.

2016

The Cubs won the World Series for the first time in 108 years.

Glossary

athlete a person who is trained or skilled in sports.

broadcast to send out by radio or television from a transmitting station.

career work a person does to earn money for living.

championship a game, a match, or a race held to find a first-place winner.

division a number of teams grouped together in a sport for competitive purposes.

Gold Glove Award annually given to the MLB players with the best fielding experience.

Great Fire of 1871 a large Chicago fire that killed 300 people and burned thousands of buildings.

induct to officially introduce someone as a member.

Most Valuable Player (MVP) the player who contributes the most to his or her team's success.

pennant the prize that is awarded to the champions of the two MLB leagues each year.

retire to withdraw from use or service.

rookie a player who is new to the major leagues until he meets certain criteria.

run batted in (RBI) a run that is scored as a result of a batter's hit, walk, or stolen base.

Silver Slugger Award given every year to the best offensive players in MLB.

triple a hit that lets the batter reach third base.

Online Resources | **Booklinks**
NONFICTION NETWORK
FREE! ONLINE NONFICTION RESOURCES

To learn more about the Chicago Cubs, visit **abdobooklinks.com**. These links are routinely monitored and updated to provide the most current information available.

31

Index

All-Star Game **22, 23, 24, 26**

Anaheim Angels **21**

Arrieta, Jake **24**

awards **20, 22, 23, 24, 25**

Baez, Javier **25**

ballparks **5, 6, 8, 28, 29**

Banks, Ernie **15, 22**

Bryant, Kris **25**

Caray, Harry **17**

Chance, Frank **18, 19**

Chicago Daily News (newspaper) **12**

divisions **4, 9, 14, 16, 25**

"Go, Cubs, Go" (song) **6**

Goodman, Steve **6**

Hulbert, William **10**

Illinois **6, 28**

leagues **4, 10, 11, 16, 23, 25, 26, 29**

Maddon, Joe **20, 21**

mascot **5**

McGwire, Mark **23**

National Baseball Hall of Fame **22, 23**

pennants **6, 14, 16, 18, 28**

playoffs **16**

Puerto Rico **25**

Rizzo, Anthony **24**

Sandberg, Ryne **23**

Sosa, Sammy **23, 29**

Sports Illustrated (magazine) **23**

teams **9, 13, 16, 21, 24, 25, 27, 28, 29**

World Series **6, 11, 14, 16, 18, 20, 25, 26, 27, 29**